HELEN MOSIMANN-KOGAN PH.D.

The Little Book of Self-Enquiry

Ancient Keys for a Modern Age

First edition

ISBN: 978-3-9525529-2-6

Cover art by Wilker Aguiar Souza

This book was professionally typeset on Reedsy.
Find out more at reedsy.com

For all seekers everywhere,
—become finders
and keep going beyond what you find
because there is always more
until everything is disguised as nothing

'Whenever I tried looking outside, instead of in, I'd be crushed by an overwhelming heaviness and sadness until I remembered again. It took quite a while for me to see that most of what goes, among so-called adults, by the name of depression isn't a disease or a defect at all.

On the contrary, it's a perfectly natural response to the pull of the divine which is always disturbing and disrupting and disorienting—straining to reorient us towards a totally different dimension.'

Peter Kingsley

Contents

Acknowledgement

My thanks to the entire cast and crew—seen and unseen—who made this production possible.

Preface

Wherever you are in your personal journey, if you were drawn to reading this book you are interested in the rich and juicy multifaceted-ness of being human. We can reflect, deliberate, rationalise, create, imagine, emote, intuit, hurt and be hurt, love and be loved.... The list of ways that we can feel, think and behave goes on and on.

However, our minds also have concealed doorways, back passages, loops and dead-ends containing surprises, illusions and delusions! We see what we want to see and what we see is not always the entire, clearest or accurate of pictures.

Self-enquiry is a lifelong journey, because the more we *do* see of ourselves, the more we find there is to see—and as we go, we correct the distortions of how we had been seeing. In time, as more distortions get corrected (usually after commitment to a journey of self-enquiry), we develop a broader perspective of all of that came before, and all that is.

There are many keys available to assist us with unlocking ever-broader perspectives of ourselves. These keys help us navigate to the unknown elements of the self, to reveal more of who we really are beyond our identities and even beyond our bodies. For the truth-seeker, there is an exhilaration that accompanies this unveiling (or onion de-layering?!) of who we really are—and once tapped into, all we want is more.

This exhilaration can come with a sense of urgency, *I have to get to enlightenment now!* until we realise self-enquiry is not a race. It is perfectly paced according to how much we can take in, how we process it and how we adjust our lives to the new realisations. There is nowhere to get to. You are yourself right now, you can find yourself as soon as you are present in your body, tuning in to the information coming through your senses. Knowing you are here, now, is the beginning of the journey / adventure / walk in the park / path less travelled that takes place within and continues... well, *ad infinitum*. That's how big the bigger picture of 'you' can get—though for this book we'll be focusing on a much smaller scale of you in this lifetime.[1]

So, welcome to this five-chapter book called *The Little Book of Self-Enquiry: Ancient Keys for the Modern Age.*

In the first chapter, we'll be looking at the nature of self-enquiry in our modern age, and how you can identify useful keys to support you in this process. In the second chapter, we'll focus on why certain ancient keys of self-discovery can be particularly helpful at this time, during what is being called the Shift of the Ages or the Awakening, or the end of times as we have known

---

[1] Check out www.thewhiterabbitreveals.com for courses that have been designed to guide and support you along the bigger-picture journeys.

them.[2]

Chapter 3 looks at how the Tarot, in particular, can help one's process of self-exploration (aside from the obvious way of doing a Tarot reading or having a reading done for you). To answer the question—Why Use Tarot For Self-Enquiry?—we will explore the mystery contained within this collection of 78 images, their esoteric purpose, how to get the most out of working with them and how they get the most out of you!

Following Chapter 3's introduction to the Tarot, the final two chapters use the major arcana of the Tarot, together with a little numerology, to answer a couple of specific questions. You don't need to have read the first three chapters to understand the last two—but it will make for a fuller experience.

Chapter 4, Which Tarot Card Represents Your Life Path?, shows you how to calculate your Life Path number, identify its associated cards and find out what this means for your path of self-enquiry in this lifetime.

---

[2] This time has been prophesied in ancient cultures and religions alike. We are seeing the 'end times' manifest in old systems being exposed as corrupt and/or failing the people, the demand for equality across race, cultures and gender, and the need for greater sensitivity and change in how we are treating the planet. Equally, this is a time that holds potential for rapid expansion of consciousness, where we awaken from the limiting beliefs we had become accustomed to repeating and transition to the broadening awareness of our potential—where we become quantum. This Shift will dramatically affect *all* aspects of our lives. The end of times as we have known them goes hand-in-hand with the beginning of times as we have never known them. This is another reason why our relationship (beliefs, expectations, fears etc.) to the *unknown* is so useful to explore at this time because it is all that lies ahead.

In Chapter 5, again using a combination of numerology and the Tarot's major arcana, we will turn to the significance of your birthday, and how the day of the month that you were born on reveals the ways you are learning to express yourself in this lifetime.

Similar to astrology and numerology, the Tarot helps us to see mirrors of ourselves from different perspectives. This can help us understand the unique blueprint we were born with, for the missions we came here to complete.[3]

Any patterns you notice across Chapters 4 and 5—and across your entire life—are useful indicators as to what makes you *you*. This makes for an objective (rather than woo-woo) approach to understanding yourself. Becoming aware, without judgement, of your patterns of thought, feeling and action is a necessary skill to develop, alongside whichever self-enquiry path(s) or key(s) you choose.

---

[3] My view is that in the one sea of everything, our soul as a higher version (dimension) of our human selves is a useful construct to work with. We have 'human lives' full of stories, drama, cycles of rising and falling, all for the soul's growth and expansion—its mission. The Shift can help us (wants us to) live increasingly as an expression of our soul rather than as our human identities because those stories have run their course (literally, we are getting tired of our own stories!). This involves redefining what it means to be human —*I am more than my story*—and this is the work of personal transformation. There are higher levels/dimensions of our soul (e.g. the Oversoul and beyond) which increasingly connect us all as one consciousness. All the dimensions, including the one in which you are reading this book, are valuable experiences in their own right and they add to the experience of the one consciousness. Being aware of the interconnectivity between all the dimensions of ourselves is to develop holographic consciousness, which we'll touch on again later.

Non-judgemental self-observation is one of the most useful skills you can develop.

Why do I keep doing this / ending up here? Why does this happen to me more than it happens to others? There must be something to this. Understanding this will help me understand myself.

Recognising and valuing your positive patterns, in terms of your unique attributes and what makes you different from everyone else, is also a critical step towards developing self-worth, self-appreciation and the biggie: self-love. Where developing self-love—as an ongoing process—has been summarised as *the one thing* that could transform our entire world into a more unified and loving place[4] (fade-in image of Superhero You).

So, although this may be a little book, it has some big messages.

Important point: The above is not to say that any interpretation of the Tarot (or numerology, astrology or any of the ancient keys we'll explore in this book) is ever set in stone; the mirrors can all be interpreted as fluidly as you allow yourself to interpret *you.*

Is your sense of self set in stone—or are you open to it being an ongoing evolutionary metamorphosis? Are you attached to what it means to be you and how you want to be perceived? Or can it be enough that you are your authentic self in any given

---

[4] *Great Human Potential: Walking in One's Own Light: Teaching from the Ninth Dimensional Pleiadians and the Hathors,* by Lee Carroll, Tom Kenyon, and Wendy Kennedy.

moment, and that's who you are in that moment—until the next moment?

One way to identify how attached you are to your identity is to see what you think about others. Do you think, 'urgh they *always* react that way', 'a leopard never changes their spots', 'that's just who they are'? Or are you open to the people in your life always showing up as who they are in the present, as opposed to who you have characterised them to be in the past? As we'll regularly come back to in this book, what you think about 'them' is a valuable insight into what you think about *you*. Where what you think about *you* is one of the most influential inputs into how you (yes *you*) create and experience all aspects of your life.

As you proceed along the path of self-enquiry you will transform the parts of yourself that you don't prefer and consolidate the attributes that you do. This means you will become more *changeable* than the rigid personality, defined roles and even caricatures you previously 'played' that had become so important—and *seemingly* safe.

Have you ever looked at yourself in the mirror a few times in one day and each time seen something different in your reflection? Or have you looked at your face from different angles, where each perspective looks like it could belong to a different face?

With all self-enquiry tools, all that matters is what stands out to you in a particular moment—in *this* particular moment, to be precise, because this is the only moment when life is happening and this is the only moment when you are this version of you.

1

Why Keys for Self-Enquiry?

First some background.

In this book, the keys we'll be considering are what have generally been called *ancient wisdom keys.* These keys come to us from historic civilisations whose philosophies and holistic perspectives of the cosmos have been immortalised in symbols and images. These keys, especially the Runes, the Tarot and the I Ching, are especially known for their use in divination purposes.

Another thing that connects ancient wisdom keys is that they all capture humanity's relationship to nature from which most of us have lost our way as a result of the separation experiment, also known as the great fall of humanity or the cosmic out-breath.[5] As such, I see the use of these keys for divination

---

[5] The separation experiment refers to the idea that our experience of separation serves a greater purpose. One way to explain this is that we have cosmic out-breaths (to separation) and in-breaths (to unity), and these cycles are as natural as your experience of breathing or a butterfly flapping its wings.

as secondary to how potently these symbols and images can awaken a dormancy in our consciousness: the parts of ourselves that fell into an amnesia that accompanied the aforementioned separation experiment. So, not only had we dis-connected from the unity of all things, we forgot that being connected was ever our reality— and our true nature!

With this amnesia, our connection to the unseen realms, our imaginations, inner stirrings and knowings faded out and seemed to be locked away as we launched ourselves head-first into physicality and materialism. 'I think, therefore I am' and 'You gotta see it to believe it' sum up how much our heads separated from the rest of ourselves.

'Head-first', in particular, refers to what became our collective approach, and now we are asking 'And what about the rest of us?'. Ancient keys have the potential to unlock and release the rest of us, this being what we *really feel* in our guts without knowing why, what we *deeply believe* in our bones without knowing how, what we *feel* in hearts and *commune with* through our spirit.

Awakening to this 'rest of us' is to become less fractured and increasingly whole, and when that happens so will more of the world we live in.

More on the ancient keys in the next chapter. Let's now take a very general look at how self-enquiry has become what it is today. What has brought us to the surging interest in the unseen parts of ourselves, when for centuries and millennia this line of enquiry was reserved for secret meetings and occult practitioners, if at all. Along these lines one may wonder:

Why is it that Ayahuasca is a tool that has been around for 3,000 to 5,000 years but no one had heard of it until the last 20 years or so?

Shamans predate sex workers as the oldest profession, but again, until the last 20 years most of the 'modern world' was highly sceptical of the ambiguous use of feathers, chanting and smoke to connect to other dimensions.[6]

The earliest ancient mystery schools date back to more than 10,000 years ago but, again, only in the last century or so, has the import of 'sacred wisdom' awakened in our consciousness.

How have we bridged the ancient knowledge not only to the present day but seen it emerge from secret and in some cases illegal gatherings, for it to now be readily available on the high street and in social media?

What follows are some historical landmarks in the timeline:

The earliest records of us awakening to the unknown parts of ourselves in contemporary society appear towards the end of the 19th century with the emergence of séances in social circles. Allen Kardec's *The Spirits Book*, published in 1857, was the first to document these events and discuss life after death, karma and mediumship. With this, the existence of and interaction with realms other than the 3D tangible one emerged into general

---

[6] In many cultures an awareness of spirit as unseen aspects of ourselves is and has always been more openly accepted than in others. At the other extreme, there are places where, still today, it has to be kept hidden under the threat of people's lives.

conversation.

Notably, in the late 1890s, Sigmund Freud (1856-1939)'s thoughts about the unconscious—thoughts we don't know we have—started to gain appeal, although his psychoanalysis as a 'therapy' would only take off much later, after World War II.

In Freud's wake, Carl Gustav Jung (1875-1961)'s development of 'analysis' included a thorough excavation of the unconscious to include a deeper evaluation of the place of symbols, archetypes, dream interpretation, alchemy and the rejected shadow. The influence of Jung's work remains prevalent today throughout the fields of psychology, psychiatry and even the New Age. Many terms like 'shadow work' and 'synchronicity' can be attributed to the work and observations of C.G. Jung.

Along a similar timeline, at the turn of the last century, the first Eastern mystics and gurus Swami Vivekananda (1863-1902) and Paramahansa Yogananda[7] (1893-1952) were establishing their teachings in the West to open hearts and minds to the ancient Vedic traditions. It would also take a few more decades for the messages from these Eastern teachers to fully sink in and together with the rise of psychoanalysis, the fashionable use of psychedelics and the increased publication of channelled material, the 1960s and '70s became the stand-out decades that they were.

---

[7] Notably, his *The Autobiography of a Yogi* has since been translated into 50 languages and has sold more than 4 million copies.

The first wave of waking from our awareness-slumber was underway.

> *"While he was writing his autobiography we were setting off the atomic bomb"*
> —From the documentary, *Awake: The Life of Yogananda* (2014)

In the meantime, the West's focus on materialism was also gathering momentum. Money, status and power were equated with being god-like. Literally. Think about the rise of the 'rich and famous' compared to our perspective of the poor and insignificant. We're still in this celebrity illusion that has somewhat mangled the spiritual tapestry and polarised our material aspirations from our personal ethics. This is reflected in the corruption that has not only permeated governments but religious and spiritual organisations, leading us to lose faith in the very places where we are supposed to find it.

With this last point we wonder, how can we maintain non-judgemental observation when we see so much that is wrong in the world. Isn't it, after all, truly *wrong*? Isn't analysis telling us what's wrong with us? Isn't the shadow dark and unpleasant?

These reflections show us how the Cold War (generally thought to span 1947-1991) mirrored the polarity within each of us. During this political era doctrines, agreements and treaties were created, borders were redrawn, partitions and walls were built all created to keep the (our) two sides apart. The political, geographical and internal landscape was becoming ever-more polarised.

Expanding our understanding of our collective and personal pasts is a large part of the overall process of breaking down the walls we have built within ourselves. This is a process that requires acceptance of all parts of ourselves and others with understanding and forgiveness, to eventually arrive at peace and wholeness.

Another way of reframing all the 'wrongness' is to consider that nothing was ever bad or wrong, but rather roles we all came to act in the great drama playing out on planet Earth that has naturally cycled between order and chaos, unity and separation. This can help us transform what we have perceived to be bad and wrong within ourselves—and our parents, governments and other leaders—and see it all differently. What have these experiences taught us and therefore *added* to our evolution, rather than what has it 'abusively' taken away from us?

This is what all keys for self-enquiry should help you with. Not only to understand yourself better but unlock new perspectives that simultaneously undo the knots of inner conflict, confusion, blame, guilt and shame by acknowledging there is a place for all experiences in the grand scheme of all things.

Rigid constructs that separate will need to dissolve into fluid perspectives that unify if we want to see positive change in the world. The big world out there and our inner world in here.

You will find that the many paths of enquiry and evaluation will lead you to one fundamental question that you may find you often return to and that is, *Why am I here?* Especially when all the wrongness is righted, then I must be here—even in this very moment where you are reading this book—not by fluke, evolutionary error, a regretful drunken night, but for some good reason.

> *"You've already made the choice, now you have to understand it."*
> —The Oracle to Neo in the movie, *Matrix Reloaded* (2003)

The journey of self-enquiry should help you understand why you chose to be here because choose to be here, you did (the last seven words to sound like Star Wars' Yoda).

Now, following that preamble, to the title of this chapter, which we will break down into two parts.

1. What is self-enquiry?[8]

It may seem obvious but let's go there anyway. Self-enquiry is enquiring into the nature of one's self, as has been encouraged across time by spiritual teachers, messengers, philosophers—and more recently, by therapists, life coaches and men-

---

[8] Ramana Maharshi (1879–1950) and Jiddu Krishnamurti (1895–1986) are two of the greatest proponents of enquiry into the self as the path to liberation. If you're serious about the self, check out their lives and works.

tors. Today we have a plethora of ways to answer fundamental self-enquiry questions such as: *Who am I? Why do I do what I do? Why do I feel what I feel? Why am I here? What brought me to this point where I am now asking these questions? Why wasn't I asking them before?*

How you answer these questions is completely up to you. You are unique! In the past, you may have sacrificed your uniqueness to belong with society, your family, etc., in fear that they would reject you for being your own person (with your own thoughts and ideas? *Gasp!*). You may have kept doing what you thought you should, to feel safe belonging with them, rather than stand up and stand out as your own—unique—self. To undo this conditioning takes a substantial amount of letting go of doing (and/or *of the way* you have done) the many things you have done to belong, be safe and be secure—or for other reasons that can be fascinating and revelatory to explore!

Once you start, you may be surprised by how much of what you do, you do because of other people and what you want their reactions to you to be. This doesn't mean you now have to strip naked and run through the streets for people to know how unique you are. Simply saying yes or no when you mean yes or no can be the easiest way to start expressing your unique self. This may sound simple, but it isn't for everyone—and it will depend on other factors, like who you are talking to and why.

The expression of uniqueness[9] permeates most modern-day societies. Consider how 50 years ago, there were only three or four channels on television, and now there are millions, even billions if you include the videos available online. Think about coffee. At the dawn of the age of coffee, there was just, erm, coffee—now we have extensive, elaborate coffee menus. We have so much customisable choice!

In the same way, the realm of self-enquiry now includes everything from orthodox religion to the New Age, NLP to EFT, dance therapists and colour therapy, through to psychedelics and silent retreats. You could say we now have extensive menus for how we can find out about ourselves. Some people just like knitting, and they find it does the job perfectly well.

2. What do you mean by a *key*?

In this little book, a *key* can refer to anything from a mentor, healer or teacher to a Tarot deck, workshop, book, the toss of a coin or lucky rabbit's foot key ring... oh, and knitting! It can be a theory or a practical approach. Keys or tools are processes and techniques that can help, by providing the scientific direction or

---

[9] Depending on your definitions, there can be a big difference between 'uniqueness' and 'specialness'. Usually, when we want to be special in other people's eyes, it's because we don't think we are. Wanting to express our uniqueness, however, has a different feel to it. It acknowledges that we are all different and equally valid and interesting in our differences. From this place, one doesn't need to 'out-special' another. This transforms 'wanting to be special' to prove something, to *knowing* that we all equally are. See what you notice from your own life. A fuller discussion on this can be found in *The Science of Acting*, by Sam and Helen Kogan or *Why We Think the Way We Do and How to Change It*, by Thomas Garvey and Dr Helen Kogan.

ambience or luck or magic or mystery—or all of these elements together—to unlock answers to deeply personal questions of self-enquiry.

Now to the full question, *Why keys for self-enquiry?*

This involves an acknowledgement that, having written two books that explain how and why we think what we think, their contents—although solid, reliable and foundational—were just that, the foundations[10]. Not to dismiss the value of those or any foundations—without them you can't build up and out, you'll only go so far before you collapse in.

- Foundations = *I know what I know.*

- Humility = *I don't know what I don't know.*

- Humility + Curiosity = *I don't know what I don't know... and*

---

[10] My first two books describe the work, my father, Sam Kogan, developed called *The Science of Acting*. That work resulted from 20 years of research, and teaching and directing students and actors. *The Science of Acting* was built upon the revolutionary ideas of Konstantin Stanislavski and Vladimir Nemirovich-Danchenko who started a search for truth and realism in acting when they founded the Moscow Art Theatre in 1898 (which my Dad would attend about 70 years later).

I'm keen to find out.

One thing that keeps us in check, despite our materialist perspectives and ideas of intellectual superiority, is that there are always things that we don't know that we don't know about ourselves—and about everything!

Until late 2019, no one (or perhaps 99.9999999 percent of us) didn't know that we didn't know about Covid-19—we didn't even know that we needed to know—and now (at the time of writing, a year and half into the pandemic) we see it has been a complete game-changer. What other things do we not know that we don't know about that could also completely re-shape our perspective of reality?

Having no idea—of what we should have ideas about—is a positive. Aside from keeping us in check, it's fuel for our personal and collective engines of evolution, because it keeps us curious, with humility.

Accepting that we don't know what we don't know about ourselves can be the initial spark to ignite our curiosity: *There are parts of myself that I have no idea about, so I am going to find out what I can.* To which we can add—*...and trust that I will always know what I need to, when I need to along this journey.*

Knowing that we will always know what we need to know when we need to know it helps to negate any anxiety that we are missing out on information critical to our survival. It also helps us release any attachment to our place in the *illusory* race to enlightenment.

This is a quantum leap from the old paradigm of *I know who I am, what is right and what is wrong and no one can tell me any different (case closed).*

In my own journey—which includes 15 years of working with individuals in a personal mentoring role, added to eight years of studying and researching neuroscience, on top of an early life immersion in *The Science of Acting*[11]—I never cease to be amazed by the multifarious input that forms our multifaceted sense of self (beliefs, thoughts and behaviours), that we have had no notion of, let alone understood the influence of. When I was studying brain sciences I came across a statistic that said that it was the most highly invested area of science, from which there had been the least return. In my career, I would say this is because we are all so unique and finding a formula that covers all our unique variations of consciousness is impossible. My view is that to be most effective, this science—of the human psyche and of human behaviour—needs to be approached on an individual basis because the inputs into who we each are are so multifarious, many of them based on utterly unique snapshots or short videos of memory from childhood.

For this, more of us need to have— and know how to use—tools to understand ourselves and for that, we need to know what we are looking for!

What follows are some examples of what makes us who we are, beyond early-life conditioning (where early-life conditioning

---

[11]   Check out footnote 10 if you missed what this is.

is undoubtedly the whopper):

- Bloodline / ancestral / family karma (the patterns or events of our ancestors that we have unknowingly been repeating)
- Parallel lives
- Future lives
- In-between lives
- Off-world and out-of-body experiences
- Near-death experiences
- Death and our beliefs about dying
- Birth and birthing
- Illness
- Soul contracts
- Ancestral trauma and wounds
- Collective agreements
- Global agendas—including political movements, wars, peace treaties and espionage
- Personal vows and creeds
- Implants and DNA manipulation
- Curses and spells
- Archetypes
- Mythology
- Religion
- How we (especially unknowingly) define and what we believe about 'god' / God, good and evil
- Extraterrestrial contact (remembered or otherwise)
- Starseed connections
- The evolutionary trajectory of humanity

There's quite a bit there, right? And I'm not saying one or the other may be influencing us some of the time, I'm saying *all* of these are influencing us *all of the time*!

Given the list above, you will understand why I recommend *using any self-enquiry key we can,* to uncover / transform / heal any unknown negative influences on our lives—because being in these end times means there are lots of them!

Next, I offer some important identifiers to help you choose a key for self-enquiry.

Identifying a Useful Self-Enquiry Key: The Six-Pronged Test

1) The key speaks to you.

Here's an opportunity to get in touch with your intuition. The tool should be something you are personally drawn to, you feel tugged or magnetised towards. See if you can trust that you have this feeling because this key can unlock something useful for you—whatever it is. Even if it is to show you why you don't want to use the key again. This is useful in itself.

It's good to be clear on how something speaks to you (gut feeling, tingles, it slaps you in the face, an angelic chorus sings as it comes to mind), rather than using a key only because someone said you should—without your own discernment.

Even if you can acknowledge *I don't know why I am drawn to X but I am*—that's a powerful indicator. With so much emphasis on rational deliberation, we've hugely undervalued intuition, especially when it contradicts 'reason'.

2) The key should be reliable; you need to feel safe and held.

If you don't trust the key, you won't be vulnerable with it and therefore get to the core of whatever you are exploring. Without trust there will be a barrier of doubt: you will hold back, cover up, remain sceptical and over-question what you discover. You will blame said key for not delivering and only later realise you weren't fully into it in the first place (taking us back to point 1).

You don't need to sign up for a ten-year membership immediately, but know that you may need some time to dip your toes in, reflect, go back and submerge a few more toes, and then later perhaps the rest of your foot. Give any tool time and weigh up the pros and cons of the experience.

Self-enquiry takes time—your whole life!—so again, remember, it's not a race. That would be like being attached to becoming detached! So if anything promises you a fast-track to enlightenment, it should raise every eyebrow in Tokyo.

The path less travelled is exactly that. Think about anything you have done that not many others have done: you do it cautiously, you check out the playing field, you get to know how it works; you want to know you are safe and that the path is in your best interest, taking you where you want to go. This applies when working with any self-enquiry tool.

3) The key should help you put pieces together across your life, not just spiritually.

This is how you know it's useful: it's helping you answer questions in your personal enquiry *and* it joins the dots of past and present everyday experiences. This is more than a cool philosophical quote or bumper sticker slogan—this is something that adds to the quality of your life; it helps you make sense of previous experiences and sheds light on current ones.

This is what can lead to revolutionary a-ha moments, as well as the minor moments of satisfaction that arise when we understand the truth of ourselves that bit better across the board. What were randomly isolated fragments of our lives join up to form a clear picture and we wholify (become more whole). This is reconnection, the very purpose of all of this self-enquiry business!

4) Check out your personal relationship with the key.

You'll want to know when is best to use it, how often and how your consciousness interacts with it. Does it feed old patterns, or help you create new, supportive ones? Are you objective in your relationship with the key or is there something you are expecting from or projecting onto it? Does some part of you want to be disappointed with it? To feel inferior to it? Special? Part of something? Lost? Could these be the reasons that you chose it?

5) A reliable key has a solid framework or lineage; it has taken substantial time to establish.

This acts as an anchor, ensuring you don't go adrift in the sea of consciousness. A self-enquiry key's reliability can be tested by how well you cope with different life experiences since you started working with it—even when you're not directly interacting with it. It is helping you become independent and confident in developing your personal sense of sovereignty. There is a solidity to the approach that works and it's reliable.

6) The key helps you unlock what you didn't know that you didn't know about yourself.

Any useful key for self-enquiry will reveal more of yourself to you, by helping you open the back door of your mind to have an honest look around; it will help you answer questions you didn't know you had. This is how you know it is helping and can continue to help you develop.

Another indicator of an effective key is that you are challenged; there are times when using it, you feel discomfort. You may feel cringy and embarrassed or it may trigger memories and emotions that you don't want to revisit. This is how you'll know it's working because it's touching on parts of your consciousness that you haven't wanted to—or haven't known how to—get close to before. With the right key, you'll find that not only can you get close to it, but you will get through it, and a few months down the line you may even forget what 'it' was.

Now that's personal transformation!

2

Why Ancient Keys for Self-Enquiry?

'Long ago in the memory of ancient man, our dreams and visions were real. We conducted our lives, raised our children and hunted our food. On top of these necessities of life, we also had a rich spirituality based on the inner world of symbols. When a young apprentice had a shamanistic vision, he knew the experience was symbolic and not literal. He also knew how to interpret that archetypal symbolism into a meaning for his own life. By allowing these experiences' validity, he acknowledged the other levels of consciousness and sought to bring them into balance with his waking self.

'Somewhere along the way we have begun to invalidate our inner world. The path of the shaman—according to the present Western world's point of view—is the path of pagans. The western world looks to these poor pagans as perhaps Third Worlders, hoping maybe one day they *will become 'civilised'. But what if we Westerners are the ones who have lost our true humanity? What if this inner world of symbols is vital to the human experience?'*

—*Lyssa Royal and Keith Priest,* Visitors from Within, Extraterrestrial Encounters and Species Evolution

The likes of Indiana Jones, *Harry Potter* and *The Da Vinci Code* have ensured that ancient codes, secrets, talismans and codices grip our interest and imagination in the modern day, as keys to the great mysteries.

Sacred sites and their historical anomalies tell us that there is more to this world than we can comprehend. Who (*really*) built the Egyptian pyramids, the Serapeum of Saqqara and its contents? Who engraved the mysteries of the afterlife and what looks to be a spaceship and an electric lightbulb in the corners, crevices and cellars of the Egyptian temples? Who (*really*) built Stonehenge, the Great Zimbabwe, the heads of Easter Island, Bolivia's Pumapunku, Mexico's Teotihuacan, the Plain of Jars in Laos, Peru's Machu Picchu, Sacsayhuamán, Chan Chan and Nazca Lines...?[12]

How did whoever built them know how to? How were technologies not available today available then? And WHY?? Why is this all here?

---

[12] If you don't know these places, look them up, scratch your head and see if you can fathom how they came to be.

19

Sorry, this book will not answer any of these questions, but it will highlight the superior intelligence and capabilities of civilisations that came long before ours. This includes histories that we will never fully comprehend unless we open our minds to the unknown (which may be a good enough reason for these places having been built, because they have brought us to these questions).

From planetary megaliths we turn to ancient wisdom keys that can help us access answers to our unknown inner worlds. Numerology, the Norse Runes, the I Ching of China and the Indian/Tibetan subtle energy system of Chakras are four such keys. We will look at the Tarot separately in the following chapters.

One important point: we are exploring ancient keys as tools for self-enquiry in the modern age, in which we are awakening and evolving towards an unknowable future. So, this isn't about doing as the ancients did, but is instead about using the teachings in a way that is relevant for where we are in our evolution of consciousness now, on the cusp of a new era.

The Runes speak to the Norse life, flora, fauna, societal structure and gods of their time. Their earliest depictions as the Elder Futhark alphabet from circa 160 CE evolve into the Younger Futhark through the Viking Age (790–1100 CE). The I Ching, which originated in the Zhou Dynasty (1045–221 BCE), has Taoist philosophy, Confucianism and familial and social norms of traditional Chinese society deeply woven into its messages. However, we don't have to live in or reproduce those times in order to experience their effect. What makes ancient keys powerful is how their timeless universal language can penetrate our modern lives to teach, guide and transform our separated parts into a wholeness.

What all ancient keys for self-enquiry have in common is that they contain the lost wisdom that the nature of the universe lies within each of us (which is what makes self-enquiry the lifelong journey that it is). These keys also understand that as the nature of the universe is a pretty big thing to explore, providing a path or structure keeps us constructively on track towards the answers we seek.

Numerology

Numerology introduces us to the power of numbers in our lives—as vibrations. It helps us frame and understand the patterns and mathematics of the universe.

Numbers and letters are a code. If we accept that *nothing* in life is random (and it can take some contemplating to reach this conclusion), then numbers and letters are codes hidden in plain sight, everywhere! Suddenly your house number, local bus route, favourite radio station, delicatessen ticket, etc. take on a new level of meaning—and so does pretty much everything else.

The three main branches of numerology today are the Chaldean system (the Chaldeans were ancient people who ruled Babylonia from 625–539 BCE), the Pythagorean school (sixth-century

BCE) and Kabbalah's Gemetria[13] system. Although these are the most prevalent today, the root origins are thought to be from 1) the Vedic teachings of India, which was orally conveyed until it started being written down in Sanskrit circa 1500 BCE, and 2) from the ancient Egyptian mystery schools[14] (of which Pythagoras would be an initiate for 22 years[15]).

The mystery schools are timeless teachings from other dimensions; putting a date on their origins brings us to the same heated debate as to when the pyramids were *really* built, and more important (I think), by whom. Conservative estimates place this at 3,000 years ago, the more liberal view is closer to 11,000 years ago.

In short, whichever way you look at it, numerology is ancient.

As we will come to discover in Chapters 3, 4 and 5, numerology is especially useful in combination with the Tarot, to explore the stages of personal development within the cycles of life.

Runes

---

[13] 'In rabbinic literature it first appears in the Baraita of the Thirty-two Rules, by Rabbi Eliezer in 200 CE. This text, which no longer exists except in references, elaborated 32 rules for interpreting the Bible. The 29th rule involved the use of gematria. Sefer Yetzirah, the earliest kabbalistic text, believed to have been written in the 2nd century CE, was the first kabbalistic text to elaborate a system of gematria.' — 'Jewish Mysticism's Origins' at www.myjewishlearning.com.

[14] *Egyptian numerology: Emergence into the Fifth Dimension*, by Sara Bachmeier.

[15] *Mathematics of Harmony as a New Interdisciplinary Direction and "Golden" Paradigm of Modern Science. Volume 1: The Golden Section, Fibonacci Numbers, Pascal Triangle, and Platonic Solids*, by Alexey Stakhov.

Recent interest in all things 'Viking' has lured many of us into the many worlds of the Norse pantheon of pagan gods.

At a time when healing the wounds of feminine victim/masculine perpetrator is so prevalent, the Norse reveal starkly different gender representation than we find in most modern-day Western societies (which are founded on the principles of patriarchal religions).

Importantly for us today, the Runes deepen our connection to and communication with nature. The seemingly basic symbols comprise (what would have been easy-to-carve) vertical and diagonal lines. Their modest representations belie the wealth they teach us about, for example, fertility, sexuality, chaos, warrior spirit, cycles of life and the quest for truth.

Across the nine Norse worlds, each deity, whether large or small—literally from a giant snake-dragon wrapped around the world to dwarves—has a unique purpose in the workings of the entire tree of life, Yggdrasill. Across these realms, we also find the mother and father are venerated equally, as are counterparts and siblings. This radically more colourful, multi-textured, intricately woven tapestry of family-life—than one father figure running the show—has much to teach us in this modern age.

Sacrifice of the negative ego-self,[16] in the pursuit of truth, is the

---

[16] The ego helps us identify ourselves as individual human beings, to live and function in 4D (with time) reality. The *negative* ego-self are the attributes of *perceived* separation that cause us and others suffering, e.g. wanting to have power over (abuse) or power under (victim).

Runes' mythological origin story—Odin went to great lengths for wisdom. He sacrificed an eye, threw himself on his spear and hung upside-down for nine days and nights to receive the wisdom of the Runes from Mímir's well. The Runes beckon us along the same spiritual warriors' journey that brought their wisdom to the world. As was asked of him, Odin asks how much are we prepared to let go of for the insights we seek. However, he is not the only one with questions for us: numerous Norse deities are peppered across the 24 symbols, each with penetrating questions for the different facets of our lives.

Not all the Runes are named after a god/goddess, but you will find many of their adventures, teachings and worlds are multi-dimensionally encrypted in these deceptively simple-looking symbols.

The I Ching

Let's say that the crux of the Shift of Ages is the dissolution of—the perspective of—separation. This means a (literally) mind-blowing, if gradual, awakening to how we have related to the world outside our skin, i.e. that none of it is outside our skin at all.
Mind-blown?

Adjusting to this change in perspective involves facing and transforming the bias, prejudice and conflict in our familial, cultural, societal and political lineages that exist within our-selves i.e. excavating our beliefs that have kept the perception of separation in place. This profound revaluation, I believe, can be achieved with a modern-day experiential[17] study of the I Ching teachings.

The 64 hexagrams (where *hexagram* means six pieces of information: *hexa* = six, *gram* = information) that comprise the I Ching are each made up of two *tri*grams (three lines of information), one on top of the other.

There are eight fundamental trigrams: Heaven, Earth, Water, Fire, Wind, Thunder, Mountain and Lake. Eight combinations of these eight *tri*grams, with one placed on top of another, e.g. Thunder above, Heaven below, gives us the 64 *hexa*grams in total.

Now consider each of these trigrams in terms of different *movements of energy*, i.e. from the stillness of Mountain to the sudden, illuminating strike of Thunder. Each element is energy moving in a unique way (*its* unique self-expression). When you combine two trigrams you are combining (one above and one below) or consolidating (when the same element is both above and below) these types of movement, resulting in further variations in the way that energy moves[18]. The relationship between the elements affects both parties and it affects an overall change, which brings us to the translation of *I Ching*

---

[17] *Experiential* because I encourage clients and students to *live* the teachings of the ancient keys not simply read or study them. Seeing the ancient wisdom keys come alive in your life is to surrender to the undulations of their rivers of awakening, healing and rebalancing. How does this happen? Check out *The White Rabbit Reveals* courses to find out more.

[18] This is without analysis of the 6 Changing Lines which adds even further detail to the picture. See any thorough I Ching resource to find out more.

as 'the book of changes'.

Back to the 'pieces of information' referring to the lines. As you can see, each line has only two possibilities: either it can be a straight line (yang) or a broken line (yin). In this way, the entire I Ching illustrates the gamut of ways in which Yang (masculine) and Yin (feminine) energies interact with each other and themselves as one: Yin-Yang.

As a key, the I Ching can unlock perspectives of unity and harmony where once there was polarity and conflict. It does this by taking us into spiritual teachings akin to tantra (which literally means *to weave,* i.e. how threads relate) and the nature of the interaction of all energies. Like tantra, the I Ching can profoundly help us understand and harmonise our relationships because its teachings are all about relating! In a world where we need slogans to tell us to be kind because we are asleep to the way our actions affect others, the I Ching has the potential to be the cohesive agent to transform fractures and friction into a fluidly functioning family—essentially within ourselves, where it *all* starts (is created and projected from).
Please understand, this is a process that takes time, kindness (!) and compassion with oneself, openness to the teachings of nature, and being prepared to make changes that effect change.

With its first publication in the late-ninth-century BCE, the text was intended to advise leaders in the management of their subjects and land. Today, the I Ching can not only deliver us to inner peace and simplicity, it can push on the boundaries of binary thinking and prepare us for multidimensional awareness.

Chakras

Easing our steadfast grip on materialism depends on developing our sensitivity, trust and relationship with the unseen, especially the unseen aspects of ourselves. Terms like 'subtle energies' or 'energy body' can provoke irritation, and questions like, 'What does that even mean?'.

However, for those that have reached their limits of pure materialism (having experienced how destructive its extremes—from poverty to privilege thinking—can be), when we awaken to the unseen we realise we have had a long-unacknowledged thirst for it. Suddenly we are interested in all things esoteric and spirituality, like we are making up for lost time. Which can lead to the self-development junkie or workshop high phase that some experience.

Arising in the early traditions of Hinduism, the Chakra—energy body—system originated in India approximately 2,000 years ago, in the ancient religious texts known as the Vedas. There, the Chakras were described as *chakravartin* or 'the king who turns the wheel of his empire in all directions from a center'—representing his influence and power, with power being the dynamic life force (chi, prana, kundalini) with which we create or turn the wheel of our lives.

Over the centuries, more detailed publications appeared, until in 1927 Charles Leadbeater, at the forefront of the Theosophical Society, wrote *The Chakras,* detailing many new attributes of the Chakras including the seven rainbow colours. Psychological and other attributes—and a wide range of supposed correspondences with other keys, such as alchemy, astrology, gemstones, homeopathy, Kabbalah and Tarot—were added later.

Although translated as 'wheels', the Chakras can be explained as energetic bridges that connect us—as separate, physical, three-dimensional beings—to higher dimensions. Or as the early traditional texts explained, Brahman, the highest universal principle, emanates into us descending through the lightest Chakra at the crown, to the densest Chakra at the root. All the Chakras can be viewed as contact points between the individual self and the one unified consciousness.

To understand the function of Chakras in our everyday lives is to understand how these bridges have been blocked by trauma, karma, emotional wounding and environmental pollution—and the effect this has on how we experience our lives. Blocked or wounded Chakras distort our perspective of reality and, unless cleared and balanced, they keep creating more of the same distortions, on repeat. Where we have been asking 'Why does this keep happening to me?'(dependent victim-perpetrator dynamic), the question becomes 'Why do I keep creating this?' (which can lead to independent and then inter-dependent sovereignty).

The system of the seven Chakras provides a comprehensive framework with which to understand our beliefs and interactions with the world. Blockages can be identified, transformation and purification take place—and a radically new life can be born.

To conclude the first two chapters, please keep in mind that self-development and self-enquiry have become big business, and it is only growing. Combined with the mega boom interest in spirituality (now that we're waking up to how thirsty we are!), people and products offer everything from dial-up cosmic enlightenment to genuine fake snake oil—for the right price. If you are starting to explore what's out there, please do so with your eyes open. You are responsible for the decisions you make, which in itself is a crucial lesson on any journey of self-enquiry.

That said, happy travels! With the right approach, you realise you can't get it wrong—and whatever you learn, it has all been perfectly orchestrated to be in your highest interest. You only have to believe that, and it will be the case.

3

Why Use Tarot for Self-Enquiry?

'True teaching is not an accumulation of knowledge; it is an awakening of consciousness that goes through successive stages.'
  —Ancient Egyptian quote[19]

We'll go into the Tarot in extra depth in this book in part to meet the interest that has exploded around the Tarot in recent years. The amount and variety of Tarot decks available these days speaks to how useful people are finding them.

Given that all things are equal, I'm always interested in what or who attracts more public attention than something or someone else at any given time. For example, why is one celebrity more

---

[19] *Egyptian numerology: Emergence into the Fifth Dimension* by Sara Bachmeier.

popular than another? What ingredients do they contain during a certain passage of time—be it for an Andy Warhol 15-minutes of fame or for decades of it—that has so many people interested in what they offer? In light of these questions, this chapter seeks to answer the question as to why you should read the rest of the book from here (as the remaining chapters are about the Tarot)—why spend any time thinking about or working with the Tarot at all?

First, a little background for the newbies to Tarot (we were all there once). The Tarot deck consists of 78 cards, 22 of which are called the major arcana, while the remaining 56 cards are known as the minor arcana. Tarot's documented origins vary but generally point to having started as Italian playing cards. On the other hand, esoteric sources reveal the major arcana to be much older—from ancient Egyptian times—and part of the mystery teachings of that era that came from the stars,[20],[21] as touched on in the previous chapter.

The major arcana depicts a journey of self-development, where the word *arcana* means 'secrets' or 'mysteries'. Each of these mysterious stages of our development, especially those depicted in these 22 cards, are also archetypes.

Carl Jung's definition of archetypes as 'inborn tendencies which shape the human behaviour' is useful to work with when dis-

---

[20] *The Ra Material: The Law of One—Session 76,* by Jim McCarty, Don Elkins and Carla L. Rueckert.

[21] *The Ra Material: The Law of One—Session 88,* by Jim McCarty, Don Elkins and Carla L. Rueckert.

cussing the Tarot. Homing in on the word *tendencies,* defined as 'an inclination towards a particular characteristic or type of behaviour', takes us to Tarot as a self-enquiry key that can help us understand our inclinations toward certain types of behaviour.

The cards reveal the patterns of thought, feeling and behaviour that are unique to us—for us to explore further. For example, getting clear on our tendencies can reveal core beliefs that we didn't know we had: *Why do I react to X Tarot card in this way? Oh, that's because I believe X represents Y.... Hmm, that's a strange thing to believe—it not only makes no sense, but this belief also makes my life complicated and causes me suffering! Why do I think my life needs to be complicated and that I need to suffer?*

This line of questioning is useful because, as is the nature of holographic consciousness,[22] beliefs aren't restricted to one area of our life—*all* of our thoughts are connected. So, if you find an unusual belief at work in one area of your life, believe it or not, you will find it (though it may take some searching) at work in others. *OMG, I think X when it comes to walking the dog, paying my bills, choosing who to vote for, at Sunday lunch with the in-laws, checking out potential hookups on my dating app.... Double*

---

[22] Term used to describe the awareness of the totality of one's environment as well as the fractals within it – and the connection between the two. Holographic images are lower-resolution (dimensional) captures of higher-resolution (dimensional) images. Note: holo*graphs* refer to this translation in images, holo*grams* refer to this same correlation in terms of information. Physicist David Bohm created the term *holomovement* to describe the fluidity within this hologram, where 'everything is connected; and, in theory, any individual element could reveal information about every other element in the universe' which he termed *Undivided Wholeness in Flowing Movement.*

OMG, I even think X when I floss my teeth!

Useful self-enquiry keys help us find a way to identify beliefs that have been affecting our thinking—that we were not aware existed. In fact, the beliefs we *don't know* are at work are the most powerful.[23] This is why being open-minded to what you don't know that you don't know is so potent.

Tarot cards, like everything else we look at, are reflections of us. We are in precise resonance with that card at the time that we pick it, and that's how we can see—or need to look for—ourselves in it. When we have a question in mind, the card we pick is in resonance with that question.

You can also look at the same card ten times and see ten different things in it (remember the looking in the mirror question?). Do remember, though: all that matters is what you see *this time*—which speaks to *who you are at this time*. That's why the following questions can be helpful each time you look at any card: they help you frame what you see.

How does the card speak to me right now? What other thoughts does it trigger? What do the colours, symbols, shapes, positions remind me of in this moment? What am I feeling in my body? How is this relevant to my current enquiry? Being completely honest with myself, what is this telling me about my current situation or question?

---

[23] *Why We Think the Way We Do and How to Change It,* by Thomas Garvey and Dr. Helen Kogan.

The Major Arcana and the Fool's Journey

You already know that the 22 major arcana cards map out a path for self-enquiry, but what can make the Tarot more accessible—and a good key to start with—is working with pictures as opposed to cryptic symbols. To help clients see holographic consciousness at work, I encourage clients to explore their worlds, daily events and interactions as symbolic pictures or tableaus that are speaking to them—how better to do that than with these illustrated 'snapshot' archetypes and learning how they come alive in one's life?

As a simple springboard to this approach, consider that the first of the 22 archetypes is The Fool, and The Fool is the *you* that takes the journey through the remaining 21 cards.

It's good to know now that The Fool *can* refer to being fool-ish and naive; more careless than carefree. However, The Fool can also refer to a childlike nature that wants to play with life, be open-minded—to explore themselves and their experiences and see where the path takes them.

Understanding The Fool in you is the starting point—then watch as The Fool travels through the remaining 21 cards of the major arcana and the aspects of yourself that they represent. Who is the constant *you* at the end of the journey and how much of *you* has fallen away?!

Where The Fool represents the beginning of a journey into the unknown, how do you feel starting any journey, project, relationship or book (?!) about which you know very little?

Sceptical? Enthusiastic? Cynical? Fearful? Excited? Oblivious? Reticent? Welcome to The Fool in you!

We can divide the remaining 21 cards into three sets of seven cards, which separate the journey into three stages wherein the individual (The Fool) explores themselves in relationship:

    1) to themselves (this includes the influence of parental figures)

    2) to life on earth (how one engages with the practicalities of life and other people)

    3) to higher wisdom beyond this world (one's relationship with the unseen: spirit, god, other dimensions, etc.)

Another perspective is that these three stages represent the development through three states of awareness:

    1) Conscious awareness

    2) Subconscious awareness

    3) Super- or higher consciousness

Being able to recognise and understand the different stages of the journey can help us as we go through our rich array of life experiences. Working with the cards can help us observe and evaluate situations. We can learn how to respond for the benefit and growth of all concerned, rather than being caught up in personal emotional reactions and judgements.

Using the Tarot with awareness and sensitivity can tap into ancient wisdoms (all the way up to the stars!) and, in turn, help you bring your universal truths to light—another aim of self-enquiry is how you authentically and creatively express yourself in this plane. In other words what and how you create!

Let's apply the Six-Pronged Test for a useful self-enquiry key to the Tarot.

1) The key speaks to you.

You are either drawn to the Tarot or you aren't—you can't force it.

2) The key should be reliable; you need to feel safe and held.

Are the cards just a bunch of pictures, or do you trust / believe / feel the reflection you are shown? Are you open to how they may be speaking with you? How vulnerable can you be with them?

3) The key should help you put pieces together across your life, not just spiritually.

Do the images, descriptions and messages help you come to tangible conclusions that connect parts of your life together?

4) Check out your personal relationship with the key.

Are you depending on the Tarot to answer your questions for you? Or are you using it as a way to develop your understanding of yourself, for yourself? Are you open to reading into all the messages, or just the ones you prefer? How do you feel when you hold a deck of cards or see images of them? Do they feel solid, intriguing? Or more like a toy and something to pass the time?

5) A reliable key has a solid framework or lineage; it has taken

substantial time to establish.

Whether you believe the Italian-playing-card or extraterrestrial origin, the cards are pretty darn old and well-established.

6) The key helps you find out what you didn't know that you didn't know about yourself.

Any useful self-enquiry key will reveal more of yourself to you, by helping you unlock the back door of your mind to have an honest look around. Do you discover new insights with the Tarot that you never would have previously considered? Do you find them revelatory? Do you feel reflective? Or untouched? Only you can answer these questions and decide if this is a path to self-enquiry for you.

Don't forget: you can always change paths down the line! Every stepping stone is only a stepping stone to the next stepping stone.

4

Which Tarot Card Represents Your Life Path?

From here on we'll be using numerology as an adjunct to the Tarot. Numerology uses your name and birth date to explain the patterns of your life. Tarot will give you more of a literal picture to work with.

If you believe it, there are no accidents, and your date of birth (next to the family you were born into and its dynamics) is one of the biggest non-accidents. In terms of numerology, your Life Path number, also known as Birth Path number, encapsulates the general thrust of your life in this lifetime. This may sound vague, but as you read through your Life Path number and that of other people in your life, you will develop an appreciation for the different themes, missions or 'programs of development' that we each signed up for.

Your Life Path can feel like a magnet tugging at you, saying,

'Hey, come over here to feel good!' The most challenging times of your life will be when you are furthest from embodying these themes, and/or when you resist embracing the challenges that *you set up* to learn what you could about these themes (accepting/understanding that you *chose* to live this life and had a say in how it would play out for the greater purpose of your soul's growth—more on this below).

This all calls for changes in perception and not taking the events of your life at face value; here self-enquiring feels more like self-investigating... *What if things are not as I think they are? What is this telling me? What is the evidence* (how things keep playing out—my patterns!) *pointing towards?*

Surrender—which can be anything from reluctant submission to an epic falling to our knees—and acceptance—that we have no idea what we are doing—radically transforms our battles with life into it being our greatest adventure / investigation / creation / work of art.

Practically, the number of your Life Path provides a valuable sign of your unique drives, values, abilities and attitudes toward other people, life and the world. It will help you understand why you have certain strengths and weaknesses and how to work with each. You'll understand why you have some of the emotional reactions you do, and why the questions that especially bug you don't bug others (hint: because they're being bugged by their own Life Path questions).

We have all come to do something with our lives[24]. With the Life Path number, what we do is not as important as *the way we do it.* A cucumber-pickler, plumber, professional poker player and prime minister can all have the same Life Path number—it's the *approach* that they develop for their fulfilment that's important here. In the next chapter, we'll look at *what* we do.

Later stages of self-enquiry, beyond the scope of this book, ask what it means to express ourselves as our soul (alongside an exploration of our soul's biography—who am I across time and space?[25])[26]. For now, the Life Path number encapsulates the awakening process, where the personality starts to make way for the soul to merge with it, through the dismantling of old constructs and conditioning—this is another way of describing personal transformation.

We will be using the Tarot alongside your numerological calculation, to add depth to your Life Path understanding.[27]

---

[24] Accepting this premise can bring to light contradictory beliefs at work that are at the root of inner conflict, like: 'life is pointless,', 'life is inherently meaningless', 'we are all just floating in space, we're born, we die and it doesn't matter what we do', 'I'm just a cog in a wheel' etc.

[25] This soul level of self-enquiry comes later, once we have a good understanding of our personality and themes we came to explore in this time and space, our current lifetime, which is exactly what the Life Path number and all keys of self-enquiry help us with. The personality weakens as we let go of the importance of our identity, eventually allowing the soul to merge and we live increasingly from a place of soul-expression rather than the former personality-identity.

[26] *The Soul Source—A Primer for Living as a Soul,* by David E Hopper.

[27] Because this is a *little* book, it is recommended that you check out fuller descriptions of the Life Paths numbers by numerologists.

A small aside: Another way to read the following material is to identify your Life Path number and read that as being of primary influence in your life. Then read all the others as also applying to you, as minor passages that you cycle through as part of your primary passage. This is most true of the number 9s, who signed up to experience all the other numbers.

Right, then, here we go.

The Life Path number is the sum of the day, month and year of your birth (using the full four numbers of your birth year), which is reduced down to a single digit.

For example:
 The birth date 12 October 1963 = 1 + 2 (= 3) + 1 + 0 (= 1) + 1 + 9 + 6 + 3 (= 19)
 Becomes 3 + 1 + (1 + 9 = 10 = 1 + 0) = 1) + 1 = 5
 Then, using the first column of the table below, you will see:
 5 = The Hierophant

Another example:
 The birth date 3 July 1982 = 3 + 7 + (1 + 9 + 8 + 2 = 20 = 2 + 0 = 2)
 Which becomes 3 + 7 + 2 = 12 = (1 + 2 = 3) = 3
 Again, using the first column of the table below, you will see:
 3 = The Empress

If you don't know the Tarot well, look up images on the internet of the Tarot card you want to know more about. There will be an array of representations, from different decks—see which one(s) you are most drawn to.

The Major Arcana

Single-Digit			
1	The Magician	10	The Wheel of Fortune
2	The High Priestess	11	Justice
3	The Empress	12	The Hanged Man
4	The Emperor	13	Death/Transformation
5	The Hierophant	14	Temperance
6	The Lovers	15	The Devil
7	The Chariot	16	The Tower
8	Strength	17	The Star
9	The Hermit	18	The Moon

19	The Sun
20	Judgement
21	The World

In this chapter, we are only looking at the first column. The Fool (0) is omitted because in this approach, The Fool is in all of us as we journey through the remaining archetypes (1-21).

What the Major Arcana Reveals About Your Life Path?

Each of the major arcana could have a book written about them, they are so multidimensional and reach into all areas of our lives in unique ways. Below is an overview of the main features as they pertain to your Life Path number.

As touched on before, how this information speaks to you specifically—as you read this—is what you need to take from it now. You may come back to it in the future and it may speak to you differently, about what you need to know then. Perspective is everything and it's always possible to change it—that's what the personal journey is all about!

Have a read about the archetypes on either side of yours, as there is often bleed-through—like being born on the cusp, in astrology. In this way, The Magician (1) and The Hermit (9) are also connected.

Life Path 1: The Magician

You are here to create in this world—to bring your insights, intuitions and ideas into the material world. Metaphysically speaking, you are bringing heaven to earth; the meaning and mechanics of this may fascinate you. This will probably take you on a journey, in your younger years, to explore what your relationship to this world is. Do you belong? Or are you an alien here? Do you prefer to observe? How do you engage?

You may have a profound experience of the void (0), as this precedes 1 and is where creation bursts forth from. This can be experienced as a deep sense of apathy or depression, where life feels empty and without meaning. You need to find meaning and authentic, empowering reasons to create. Along the way you will have many experiences of what you *don't* prefer or want to create, as well as brief glimmers of what is possible—keep following the glimmers, without expectation or attaching to what you think your creation means or what it means about you.

As you explore your relationship to the world, you will need to face your fears of being number one. You will need to overcome your resistance to standing out from the crowd, of having opinions that are different—and be ready to create anyway. A sense of emptiness will always be present if you only do what others do to feel safe or accepted, even though this may feel comforting at first. Your success will be found in identifying your uniqueness and valuing the uniqueness of others. Success is found in recognising that everyone is number one to themselves, and fulfilment can be found in helping other people realise this.

Life Path 2: The High Priestess

How you receive and connect to your insights is of great value. So too is measure and balance. What you do with your insights and how they influence and are integrated into your material life and physical relationships is at the crux of this path.

Do you separate sections of society as being this or that, approving or disapproving of them?

Although you may try to hide it, do you have a nagging voice that says your way is better than others', only to swing to the other side and feel desperately worse than others? Do you separate what you intuitively know from how you live? Have you sat with how that feels? Can you commit to finding balance and integration?

Your pining for harmonious relationships will take you through a journey of experiencing, understanding and healing conflict. This is to seat you, as The High Priestess, at peace between the two columns representing all the negative and positive forces in the universe. Equally she sits, in serenity, between intellect and spirit; here all conflict is resolved.

Your place is to be equidistant between dualities, to establish the trinity—the third point of an equilateral triangle. You see both sides equally. Harmony and equanimity are of paramount importance in your life. Your journey to reach this point establishes the foundation upon which insights transform from being dreamy, escapist and whimsical, into foresight, vision, direction—and establishes the universe as all-inclusive!

Life Path 3: The Empress

The mother of the set, being nurtured and nurturing others is your cornerstone, which likely means you have had disturbing, if not debilitating, early life experiences. Your path is a deep evaluation of the nature of love in general, and unconditional parental love specifically.

Childhood experiences of neglect/abuse will ask you to completely deconstruct and then reconstruct—for yourself—the meaning of guidance, support, nurture and nourishment. This will ask for profound understanding and forgiveness of others and a complete letting go of (coming to peace with) the past to be present.

In turn you will gradually develop a new connection with the earth you walk on and how you relate to your body. Connecting to the earth and its cycles of growth, abundance and decay will help you embody flexibility and, more importantly, compassion. Compassion will become the staff that you keep gripped close to your side.

As you evolve into The Empress, controlling behaviours will no longer be destructive; you'll be able to watch them gently dissipate. Acceptance, allowing and *flow* eventually become your M.O.. This will transition you to *your* new definition of parenting and teaching, where abundance (rather than a financial quantity) as a natural right for all souls, is yours to emanate as an example to others.

You will have learned that how and what you communicate to others can either create or destroy—it can be loving or hateful, or desperately confusing. Can you love unconditionally through your words—by loving yourself clearly and unconditionally first?

Nurture, kindness and care are the keys to your abundance, all starting with yourself.

Life Path 4: The Emperor

Authority, structure, order, reason—your journey will ask you to regularly review your experience of these terms in the patriarchal era and transform them, evolve them, rebirth them.

Submission, chaos, vulnerability and intuition are four branches of this path that you will need to journey through for the metamorphosis to be complete. In your death and resurrection, you have the potential to birth a new world, though it will take time and this itself requires becoming friends with time.

The challenges of this path are unique in that you will be actively engaged in a purification of your mind, which can only be achieved when you are ready to surrender it—and the illusion that it is, or ever was, under your control. This means letting go of your definitions, letting go of being right, letting go of holding it all together—because what you have held on so strong to was rooted in a belief that you do not want to keep perpetuating. The belief was/is that the world is not a safe place.

To let go is to trust in dimensions beyond the mind and the material world—to float in the ethers among the puppet strings being pulled by the gods. But you cannot remain here: this will lead to anarchy, and you are here to build, not destroy. So back to earth you come, with wisdom for a new way. It will be coherent, practical and necessary. Your transfiguration of authority, structure, order and reason will be imbued with the valour, wisdom and gentleness required to create a new foundation for self, greater freedom for family and a new fabric for society.

Life Path 5: The Hierophant

Teacher and student: you have established principles about these roles that have influenced your life profoundly. Your experience of teaching environments—school in particular but also religious or other curriculum education—held significant sway over you, having created set ideas about what it means to teach and what it means to study, what it means to follow and to be followed and even what it means to manipulate and be manipulated.

As you delve into self-enquiry, this area of your life has much to show you about leadership and helplessness, and what you have thought of both. Your fulfilment arrives as you dissolve the helplessness that has kept you following external guides, in order to find your guide within—your spirit and your body. New/alternative teachers will come your way to teach you how to 'be one's own teacher' and this will take an extensive period of trial and error, testing and evaluating how you teach yourself and how you can learn from yourself.

Similar to The Emperor, The Hierophant can represent out-of-date representations of authority. Separation of your mind (which can be overactive) from your body and spirit is your challenge to bridge—can the teacher and pupil swap places and the mind listen and learn, while the body and spirit inform and even instruct? Can teaching and learning be infused with fun, freedom and spontaneity and at the same time develop discipline, curiosity and critical thinking?

Finding your answers in the still place of being both teacher and student simultaneously, again like The Emperor, has the potential to restructure entire societies. Because of the hefty questions being asked, it may take until your later years to maturely answer them and then see those answers materialise.

Life Path 6: The Lovers

The focus here is on the illusion of 'the other'. As we integrate a holographic understanding[28] of the world, we move through the shock of waking up to there being no 'other'; that our Lovers are ourselves, who we see in the mirror.

To walk the path of The Lovers is to be prepared to see ourselves from every angle, every day, in every person close to us, with no resistance, shame or anger. And eventually as an experience of hanging out with yourself in a multitude of manifestations.

If you look at the image of The Lovers card next to The Devil card, you will see many similarities, because The Devil can be The Lovers' shadow or underworld. This Life Path has the potential to deliver one to serene, buoyant and even euphoric states of connection to everyone and everything—realisation. Although to get here, one will have to clear The Lovers through The Devil's playground of addiction, dependency, hedonism, subconscious confusion and conflict.

The way out is through another. It is the winning ticket to solving the separation experiment and the principle reason why Source / God / the Absolute created the 'other': to expand itself. The inner sacred marriage is to live this understanding. Yes, love is the fabric of creation, and yes, self-love is one of the greatest lessons we have all come here to learn—and love through the embrace of the other as the self is a wisdom key that will unlock the higher dimensions of your heart.

---

[28] 'The ability to be aware of both the totality of the environment as well as the particulars within it.' —Marshall Lefferts, in *Cosmometry: Exploring the HoloFractal Nature of the Cosmos.* Holographic understanding is a scientific reference to the indisputable awareness of the interconnectivity and oneness of all things, where the All exists in each part it is comprised of.

Life Path 7: The Chariot

Sometimes depicted holding the reins of one black and one white horse, you are destined for a path of taming, steering and uniting opposites for success. This will involve accepting paradox; relinquishing the pride of being the best and the shame of being the worst at the very same time. Then see who remains! For this is the real you, to ride your chariot to physical and spiritual success.

Until this time, while you bounce from one half to the other of any opposite (good / bad, saint / sinner, etc.), you will always feel a discomfort in yourself. Be aware of that discomfort: it's the barometer of your progress and should only be used in this way, rather than as a reason to self-harm through comparison, judgement and criticism.

When your horses are aligned, you'll be able to ride across increasingly larger stretches of land—be it literally through travel, or productivity, or vibrant enthusiasm to create and share.

Recognising the validity of all perspectives, especially whichever you have in any moment, aligns you with The High Priestess—who is your equal opposite in her stillness. You are defined, however, by fire and the actions of charging towards success, when you embody acceptance with form and freedom.

Finally, whether you travel physically or through your inner worlds, you will simultaneously be able to exist in the still is-ness [29] of the present.

Life Path 8: Strength

Strength has traditionally meant power, protection, defence and destruction. Your path will take you to the root of these concepts, to see how they were seeded in fear and grew into an armour of protection. This will have manifested physically in your physique, how you hold yourself—or in the distance you keep yourself from intimacy.

But the key to great Strength is acknowledging the value of vulnerability.

When you recognise that the distance you keep from others is kept in place by the disconnection within yourself, your world pivots on its axis. In this moment alchemical transfiguration takes place, only possible when fire meets water. Your outward-facing personality has touched your soul and the infinity symbol connects the two.

When this moment of submission takes place, and it may happen numerous times in your life, your inner vision will take precedence over your outer. From this point, you will be guided from your heart, not from your thoughts, nor your 'knowings', nor your graspings. This is the embodiment of your lionheart.

---

[29] The 'is-ness' refers to the place of awareness—that can be sustained for anything from a few seconds and hours to months, years and decades—where all differentiation falls away. It can also be referred to as zero-point, realisation, acceptance, pure being, pure presence – even liberation.

The love that emerges for yourself in these moments of surrender, accompanied by a fierce will and determination, creates a strength that can move mountains with little effort.

By continuing to *respect* your sensitivity, not crushing it, overriding or numbing it, your appreciation for love grows. That is to say, you keep falling in love with love itself: for its gifts of healing, expansion, and its nature *as* existence, creation and experience itself.

Like the parable of the competition between the Sun and the Wind to see who was strongest and could get the human to take their coat off—it wasn't Wind, who only made the person hold on to their coat tighter, but the Sun, who only had to shine, and the human gladly removed their outer-garment.

This parable asks, so what do you think real Strength is now?

Life Path 9: The Hermit

Establishing the light within, to shine it out in the world. As number 9, you contain all the preceding numbers ($1 + 2 + 3 + 4 + 5 + 6 + 7 + 8 = 36$, $3 + 6 = 9$; or, $1 + 2 + 3 + 4 + 5 + 6 + 7 + 8 + 9 = 45$, $4 + 5 = 9$).

Your life path may start—in your early years—with more introverted reflection, as you consider the breadth and depth of yourself. You watched those around you with a mixture of wonder and bemusement, and you developed a strategy to survive what may have felt like life in an asylum.

In later years, your understanding and transforming the result of early-life experiences of suffering delivers you to a broader, deeper and more compassionate view of all people and of all life. Along the way you establish an intense and philosophical nature, which can be 'all or nothing' in your approach. As this 'all' becomes tempered and the 'nothing' is awakened, your deliverance is to wisdom unparalleled.

Are you in or out of your cave? Can you be both, keeping your inner flame firmly alight while you interact with the outside world? (like the serene Chariot, who is still even while moving).

Your introverted nature is best used, rather than *hiding from* the world, as a time to *prepare for* the world—because the world waits to experience the results of your sacred cogitations.

As you balance your beliefs about justice and equality, through your own transformation you become ready to emerge as a voice that can communicate your vision for everyone, to everyone. The brightness of your inner light can light up the path for others now—because you recognise how you have embodied and continue to embody them all.

5

What's the Significance of Your Birth Day?

In this chapter, we will look at the number of the day that you were born on as an indicator of *how* you—what you do to—express your inner world to the larger world. We will still use numerology, in terms of how the vibration of the number of your birth day correlates to a journey through the corresponding numbers in the major arcana, but no calculations will be necessary as they are contained within the chart.

In the previous chapter we looked at the path of your life: out of the nine different paths, which is specific to you and your transformative process (with an eye on all of them as stages of the path within your path).

From the early chapters of this book, you may have understood that the antidote to living, solely to feel safe and belong, the way others (predominantly our parents, but also family and society) do is to nurture one's unique self-expression (without having to strip naked and run through the streets!)—and that's precisely what your birth day number can help you identify.

To optimally express your unique self includes consideration of the following:

- Your innate gifts
- Your personality characteristics
- Instincts in relationships
- Ideal career environment
- Ideal circumstances around finances

Identifying your number and the associated major arcana cards reveals a fascinating road map of learning to express your truest self which considers the above bullet points.

To repeat what was stated earlier, there is no race in self-enquiry, and so although there is a map, this doesn't mean that it's about getting to the end of the route as quickly as possible. With the goal-focused filters of modern-day life, we need to remember the value of process—and that there is never *really* an end. Again, it's here and now, here and now, here and now, when your whole life is happening.

With this in mind, observing and enquiring as to *how and why we do things* eventually becomes as (if not more) enriching than gaining the certificate, launching the product, increasing the bank balance, influencing your followers, etc. With this approach, we value the continuous experience of becoming. A (male) shaman friend once remarked that the *Big Bang* is a term that must have been coined by a man[30]; a woman would have called it the *Gentle Blossoming.* Recognising and appreciating the fact that we are all *always* Gently Blossoming as opposed to only being successful when we achieve a Big Bang, is a way to value and love ourselves far more than we have. Which, to repeat, is all we *really* need to do to change the world—if that's something you want to do.

Using the Chart

Find your birth day number and note the row it is on. Consider all the cards (whether two or three) in your row as relevant, depicting a passage of experience, consolidation and evolution. The details of each row are explained below.

To clarify before we proceed, your Life Path number (previous chapter) reveals the overarching themes of this lifetime, which includes transforming the distortions or woundings of child-hood to reach your X-marks-the-spot of personal fulfilment.

Where the Life Path number is about *your approach to becoming,* the birth day number is *the actions you take in the world that correspond to this emergence.* There will be many crossovers, however, do also note the distinctions: My Life Path number *is my approach to what I do* (birth day number).

---

[30] Which it was. It was first said by Fred Hoyle in 1949 to refer to Monsignor Georges Lemaître, who originated the theory. The story goes that Hoyle saw Lemaître and called him 'The Big Bang Man'.

The Major Arcana

1 The Magician	10 The Wheel of Fortune	19 The Sun	28 -
2 The High Priestess	11 Justice	20 Judgement	29 -
3 The Empress	12 The Hanged Man	21 The World	30 -
4 The Emperor	13 Death/Transformation	22 -	31 -
5 The Hierophant	14 Temperance	23 -	
6 The Lovers	15 The Devil	24 -	
7 The Chariot	16 The Tower	25 -	
8 Strength	17 The Star	26 -	
9 The Hermit	18 The Moon	27 -	

In this chapter, we are looking along the rows of the chart.

The Ones (1st, 10th, 19th, 28th)

Innovators, pioneers and leaders.

You prefer to work independently; to have the freedom to develop innovative ideas and forge new ground. You enjoy time to yourself and value independence in others. When you have cultivated your interests and skills, you are the one to make things happen and lead by example.

The Magician represents the beginning, the entrepreneur that will get things done. Because what you introduce is often the first of its kind, you need the freedom and confidence to live a couple of steps ahead of others; with a broader picture of what is happening and why, and what needs to come next.

Hence, **The Wheel of Fortune** and its turning through cycles is significant for your overall development. These passages include the closing of chapters that served to ignite you on your path, but that need resolution and closure for you to move on. You consider your past in light of your present, and both together in light of a new and distinct future. This helps you discern what you need and what you can leave behind. This bigger-picture perspective extends to your endeavours. You understand what brought things to the here and now and what needs to take place next, to take your endeavours where they need to go—and this insight ensures that your futuristic creations see the light of day.

Cue: **The Sun**—the bright shining orb that warms and nourishes. You don't care about impressing people, however you are recognised for bringing joy and enthusiasm to other people's lives, through your pioneering ideas made manifest. Your actions help people feel good.

Be aware of being: aloof, lazy, proud, shy, narrow-minded, indecisive, aggressive, self-conscious, stubborn.

The Twos (2nd, 11th, 20th, 29th)

Acutely sensitive, empathic, and observant; your greatest fulfilment comes from working in psychological, artistic, spiritual or healing fields.

With a heightened 'two' energy, men can often unabashedly express themselves in a more sensitive and artistic way, and all genders flourish when immersed in nature and the raw experiences of life—despite at first feeling resistant to them and wanting to remain in control. **The High Priestess** is a clear representation of the inner sight, that knows without needing to justify, explain or defend their knowing. You just do.

Cue: **Justice**! It just-is—a nice example of the cultivated expression of the number two. When the scales of right and wrong (and all other polarities and contradictions) are balanced, truth and clarity are expressed sharply as the sword of truth. The adjusting and balancing of opposing views is a crucial and ongoing element of your life. The more you cultivate this skill, bringing harmony to conflict, the more the sword of clarity can be used to support others. Whatever you do you need to do it, and be an example of it being done, fairly and in balance.

And, as **Judgement** depicts, you can help others rise from the slumber or stagnancies of their lives, as you did for yourself. This is the uplifting nature that your light-heartedness contributes to other people's lives—enriched by the time you take to listen and assess, before proposing your suggestions or sharing your insights which could (positively) rock their lives.

Be aware of being: careless, scattered, meddling, insecure, easily hurt, extremely emotional or conversely completely numbing yourself from your feelings.

The Threes (3rd, 12th, 21st, 30th)

Expressive promoters, communicators and enthusiasts.

The Empress depicts the artistry of nature. This is simply nature's way: it is artistic and beautiful. And your enthusiasm and expressive nature are simply your way—you are abundant with it! A fundamental passage for you is discerning what you are authentically interested in (*why* are you enthusiastic about it?) and refining how you express this excitement, for it to be clear in your own mind and of greatest value to others.

The Hanged Man illustrates the passage of being turned upside down as you take time out to slow down and deeply consider your authenticity. This delivers you to a new vision of reality, one that incorporates a deeper understanding of the ways of the world, by developing a deeper understanding of yourself. This passage may feel stalling or like your momentum is being stifled, but in fact this is a valuable investment into your great potential which will realise at the perfect time....

For what awaits you is **The World.** You can see **The Empress** as the microcosm to the macrocosm of **The World**. Therefore, you are encouraged to contemplate 'bigger' and 'all-encompassing' at the same time as the implications of your words and actions in your everyday life. Bridging these two perspectives takes acceptance of and finding the value in your **Hanged Man** passages of patience and fine-tuning. This is the crucial key to unlocking it *all*, because **The World** illustrates the influence you are capable of.

Be aware of being: judgemental, deceptive, flippant, scattered, complacent, moody.

The Fours (4th, 13th, 22nd, 31st)

Builders, doers and managers, re-creators.

You are influenced—for better or worse—by the family, house and home; both positive and negative experiences can either fuel or swamp you. With **The Emperor**'s overseeing attributes, you give shape to ideas, and ensure all components are accounted for, quality-controlled and functioning at their optimum.

During the global shift away from the weight of patriar-chal influences, you will face significant experiences of **Death/Transformation**—your own and others'. There is no way around these experiences if you want to progress. They will take substantial periods of reflection and integration, for you to find the keys that lay therein (similar to the Three's needing the Hanged Man). This transformation, in turn, unlocks the architectural designs of what you *really* came here to build—or, more appropriately, *re*build from the ashes of the old. In this way you are a pivot-point.

The **Death/Transformation** passages will be experienced in a particularly intense way, to introduce adaptability and fluidity to what could otherwise be an unbalanced, rigid and traditional nature (walls and boxes!). Once you have passed through these portals of metamorphosis, what you build will be strong and necessarily fluid enough to contain hitherto unforeseen expressions of consciousness.

Be aware of being: outspoken, idealistic, narrow-minded, too serious, insistent on what you resist—and resisting anything

61

new or uncomfortable.

The Fives (5th, 14th, 23rd)

Movers and shakers, pollinators and promoters.

This card/number partnership tells us a lot about how **The Hierophant** (or The Pope, as this card was originally termed) has distorted over time—reflecting our changing perspectives of organised religion. First, **The Hierophant** or Pope are both, in their original form, pollinators and promoters of God's word, let's say. However, we rarely see them as movers and shakers. When we do, however, we see that *how they inspire others* is their real key to success, even more than what they are saying.

We lose faith (pun intended) when we see spiritual leaders reciting the same words and rituals repeatedly, without meaning or substance. Especially when actions and behaviours in a temple don't align with the temple's teachings: hypocrisy. For any Five to attain fulfilment, it's not *whether* you evolve through the stages of the Fives but that you have to!

Education is another example of organised teaching—through the pollinators and promoters of ideas. **The Hierophant** can depict being taught or guided by a wise one; and yet, again, education systems fail children and families if they are not holistic, adaptable and the teachers a living example of being inspired by life with their own enthusiasm to learn.

Temperance is not an option, it's a necessity. For the Five to blossom in this age of global change, you must adapt to the times, be open to new ideas, empathically connect to your audience, travel physically or through a variety of perspectives to create with freshness, colour and brilliance. Similar to the Four path, that must go through Death/Transformation to fully emerge, here Five is obliged to integrate up-to-the-minute vibrancy, in all areas of life, to be an original and dynamic way-shower for others.

Be aware of being: careless, indecisive or a procrastinator, irresponsible, thoughtless, reckless, impulsive.

The Sixes (6th, 15th, 24th)

Nurturers, counsellors, healers.

The home, family and harmony are vital ingredients to your success. This is depicted in **The Lovers** as the meeting of opposites in harmonious union. 'Harmonious union' are two simple words that contain within them years of process, understanding, humility, patience, strength, wisdom and many more ingredients required to establish balanced and healthy relationships. The Lovers live love and yet many of us are stumped at Go, and what the L-word even means?

For this reason and to achieve success in this, you will traverse the teachings of **The Devil** within yourself to get there. The Devil is not about being bad, nor is not about hell, although there may be times when life feels like this. It's within **The Devil** that we learn to heal, which is your training for the services (love) you

63

will offer others. Here you will learn to integrate differences, so that you can flourish, create, nurture and thoroughly enjoy the pleasures of life. **The Devil** speaks of hedonism, codependency, conflict, being emotionally controlling (and projecting this onto others), having high expectations of yourself and others, that cause you to feel let down and/or that you are letting others down.

The Devil usually depicts people in chains, in what looks like a cellar or basement. These are the subconscious psychological bindings you are to free yourself from—it is your passage and what makes you such a good counsellor. You will need to explore how 'unconditional' fits into the experience of love, how this was lacking in your upbringing, and therefore why it is so important that you integrate this into your relationship with yourself. You are here to love, nurture, heal and serve, and the only way you can do that for others is to have practiced, practiced, practiced and perfected this with yourself. This will always transform conflict into harmony, resentment into invitation, rejection into embrace.

Be aware of: overstretching or complacency, right/wrong or punishment/reward thinking, self-deprecation or hiding yourself away, dreamy or nostalgic ideas of perfection versus objectively facing life in the present.

The Sevens (7th, 16th, 25th)

Knowledge-driven truth-seekers, compelled by unique per-spectives of spirituality and the workings of the universe, you

enjoy working alone.

However! These changing times will not allow you to rest in the comfort of a library for the rest of your days. **The Chariot** indicates the necessity for movement, confidence and expansion. The Age of Aquarius is the information age—how can information be put to the best use for all of humanity? How will you do it? You are warned against complacency and getting too comfortable in your mind (or your armchair), and are asked how you will deliver and make manifest—for The Charioteer can be the one that leads an army, shouting words of encouragement and determination to defeat the enemy.

The Tower, as your passage, exemplifies breaking through the ivory tower of solitary study or contemplation, so as to charge your revolutionary ideas into the world. You have the power to dramatically awaken—and so your journey is to be mindful of when you fall into slumber. For when your ideas and perspectives are grounded in their practical implications for humanity, they become a solid beacon to inspire and light the way for armies. The Tower also represents the home and old institutions; how these have limited your perspective will need breaking down for you to break through.

Be aware of: how and what you communicate (too little or too much); being sceptical or critical, living in the past, repressing your emotions in favour of your mind; living in a dream world, disconnected from others and/or in judgement of them.

The Eights (8th, 17th, 26th)

Authorities, executives and leaders.

These are some of your extraordinary potentials. But like the Sevens, you also have a strong 'However!' in the mix. In these changing times, your experience of authority figures and leaders in your childhood may be in stark contrast to what they need to mean for you now and in the future. Your **Strength** will develop by filtering and deciding what hard work and ambition mean to you. You cannot do what has always been done (or how you saw it being done)—you have to find *your* way of doing it. Discipline, vision and sense of purpose will carry you through, but you have to decide to what end. Why do anything? Who are you doing it for? Until it is for yourself and your fulfilment, you will be resentful of others and you don't carry grudges well....

The lion is usually depicted in the **Strength** card—it represents the ego. For this king of the cats to be tamed, it first has to be understood. *Who am I?* and *What am I doing?* are questions that you will keep coming back to until you are not ashamed of the answers.

When you are happy with yourself and your place in the world—you are blessed with **The Star**. For the success of an Eight comes not from aspirations in the material world but from alignment to the unseen world—be it of the stars, Great Spirit or simply your soul. The universe wants you to shine unashamedly, for reasons that you are proud of—and shoot across the sky as an example of what is possible.

Be aware of being: materialistic, manipulative and controlling, careless with money, thoughtless, inconsiderate of others (self-consumed), angry, resentful.

The Nines (9th, 18th, 27th)

Spiritual leaders, humanitarians and holistic practitioners, you have come to make a difference to the world.

The Hermit indicates significant periods of seclusion as you craft your understanding, skills, approach and direction. This can bring with it the tendency to be over-separatist, which takes you in the wrong direction, because all-inclusive is the thrust of your journey. In the darkness, like **The Hermit** holding up the lantern in their cave, you will find the light. For extensive periods and various reasons, you will be taken deeper into the dark, to find your way and to know that you can always find your way back to the light. Eventually you will know you can live in coexistence with both, simultaneously. Cue your Eureka moment and that which is illumined by **The Moon**! How similar **The Hermit** and **The Moon** are!

The less difference you see between the dark night of the soul and the dawn of enlightenment, the more ready you are to rise like a full moon on a dark night—and light the way, finding the answers and a vision for the future. 'Your job is to attend to the soul of humankind'.[31] **The Moon** can speak of over-emotionality, wallowing in moods and to great depths. However, when you recognise its watery nature as your gift and understand how it guides you up dimensional spirals of

---

[31] *Success by the Numbers,* by Carol Adrienne.

67

understanding (rather than round and round in circles, chasing your tail), you will rise from the tides as a solid constant for all that have eyes to see you. At this stage it won't matter whether you are seen or not seen—your message is being delivered and that's what you came here to do.

Be aware of being: resentful, a perfectionist (and expecting the same of others), gullible, easily manipulated, oversensitive, isolationist; comfortable in suffering.

6

Conclusion

'We have a syncretic predilection and like to combine various teachings and traditions together. This reflects the breaking down of barriers which is part of the global age that is beginning to dawn. While such open-mindedness is helpful in expanding our horizons, it is not without its limitations. Trying too quickly to combine spiritual teachings and traditions can be like trying to grow oranges, apples and bananas on the same tree—while it sounds like a good idea, it cannot work. A spiritual teaching develops organically and cannot be artificially combined with another, even with good intentions. A sampling or preliminary exploration of different teachings should not be equated with a real understanding growing out of a serious practice. There may be any number of good spots to dig a well, but only if one digs deeply in a single place will one really find water—and only if one digs in a place where there is water.'

—*David Frawley,* Tantric Yoga and the Wisdom God-
desses

At the start of this little book, the message was these are
(r)evolutionary times in the realms of self-enquiry, so use any
help you can get. This may have sounded over-simplistic or even
flippant. However, if you agree (or are open to trying out the
idea) that there are no accidents in existence and if everything
is energy existing as frequency and vibration then whichever
self-enquiry key you are drawn to, must be the one that matches
your frequency at the time you are drawn to it. This says, you
must be ready for it now—*whatever* it is.

Then, if, as and when your frequency significantly changes you
will either go to a new level with that key or you find you are no
longer in resonance with that key and the (literal and emotional)
attraction to that key falls away.

The recommendation to go with any tool you are drawn to is an
easier way of saying all the above *and* it's a curious and fun way
of seeing what's out there that you are in resonance with at any
given time. *Did you ever think you would enjoy knitting or benefit
from carrying a lucky rabbit's foot or exploring Tibetan mysticism?*

Bear in mind, being in resonance with something doesn't mean
you will always like what you attract, it means that there are
sufficient similarities to draw you together at and for a particular
time. *Did you (really) think you would enjoy knitting or benefit
from carrying a lucky rabbit's foot or exploring Tibetan mysticism*

forever? Are you open to being attracted to something else weeks or years later that is more in resonance with who you are then? How changeable are you? How changeable is the key you are working with?

You can also be attracted to several keys at the same time. You may dig for water in one place and find there is a spring, while in another spot you only find infrequent drops and yet both serve you equally well for now. As you keep digging, you may find you want more of X and less of Y; this discernment keeps you exploring what is *most* in resonance with you. One day you may find a well—which does not necessarily mean this well will always be your well; you may tire of the taste of its water or it may dry up when you realise you have drunk as much as you can from it.

After some time, the novelty of trying out different drops, springs and wells can wear off. You have narrowed down what you could take from each and decide that you want one flowing river that you can build your house next to.

River found, and house built. At this stage, you probably have a pretty good handle on who, what and where your self is, while being open to that perspective changing. You realise that self-development, spirituality, self-enquiry *and* being a grounded human being with a multidimensional consciousness who is fully integrated in the material world are all the one same (cohesive) thing. You have tools, keys and methods that you have tried, tested and trust to help you navigate the more-challenging passages of life in the 21st century, and you draw upon them when you know you need to.

71

Self-enquiry, at this stage, is no longer something you are interested in on the side. *It is you*, in every moment, with all of life, the world you walk around in and the people you encounter. You're interested in all of it!

The river you live beside is your personal river of truth, it's a frequency you recognise easily. It doesn't belong to one school of philosophy or another—it belongs to you. When something is true to you, you know it, and when it's off, it feels like walking with a piece of gravel in your shoe. You are not afraid of or overwhelmed by the next truth; you know it's not a threat, judgement or criticism of your nature, it's just the next truth. You now know how to incorporate new truths into who you are and how you want to explore and express them.

Yes, self-enquiry is a lifelong journey because there is always more to experience and learn, and during these paradigm-shifting times we never know when the next Pandora's box will open. In the early years/decades the journey of self-enquiry can feel especially turbulent, because paradigm shifts ask (demand?) us to shed *all our ideas* of what it means to be who we are—and this is a mighty task, because humans have accumulated a lot of ideas (that we are finding out to be nonsensical, let alone untrue) about ourselves from our colourful and convoluted history.

Eventually, however, we get used to our new understanding of what it means to be an ever-changing soul-infused human at this time; we carry less baggage, making it easier to go with the flow. We are open to our minds being regularly blown; we can integrate the implications easily and move on to the next experience. We become lighter all the time, which is a much truer definition of who we are and all that we see—light.

This book was written to provide you with some new perspectives on self-enquiry in the modern age and to introduce you to *The White Rabbit Reveals (TWRR)*. TWRR is an organisation that was created to help reveal more of you to you using a variety of ancient keys and modern insights.

Our purpose: to help you build *your* unique home next to *your* river of truth: a river that connects you with all others and the big ocean of everything.

–

And with those final words, I want to thank you for your interest in this material, my work and the services we offer at The White Rabbit Reveals.

By way of thanks, I would like to extend a gift to you of 20% off either the three- or six-month Open Course mentoring with any of our consultants.

To find the details head to The White Rabbit Reveals website and navigate to our « Beginners » courses. Scroll down and there you will find a link to « Open Course Mentoring » and links to schedule a free potential client call to discuss this opportunity further.

When you are set on who you want to work with and for how long, here's your code for the checkout: Iwanttogofurther88

Bibliography

40 Verses on Reality, by Ramana Maharshi (2015), SOHM Publishing

A Book of Life, by Peter Kingsley (2012), Peter Kingsley Publishing

Cosmometry: Exploring the HoloFractal Nature of the Cosmos, by Marshall Lefferts (2019), Cosmometria Publishing

Eastern Body, Western Mind, by Anodea Smith (2004), Celestial Arts

Egyptian numerology: Emergence into the Fifth Dimension, by Sara Bachmeier (2018), Balboa Press

Great Human Potential: Walking in One's Own Light: Teaching from the Ninth Dimensional Pleiadians and the Hathors by Lee Carroll, Tom Kenyon, and Wendy Kennedy (2016), Ariane Editions

Looking Glass Universe: The Emerging Science of Wholeness, by John P. Briggs, PhD, and F. David Peat, PhD (1984), Simon & Schuster

Runelore: The Magic, History, and Hidden Codes of the Runes, by Edred Thorsson (1987), Weiser Books

Self-Actualising Cosmos: The Akasha Revolution in Science and Human Consciousness, by Ervin László (2014), Inner Traditions

Success by the Numbers, by Carol Adrienne (2018), Spiral Path Publishing

The Book of Thoth, by Aleister Crowley (1981), Samuel Weiser, Inc.

The Collected Works of J. Krishnamurti, by Jiddu Krishnamurti (1991), Kendall/Hunt Publishing Company

The Complete I Ching, by Taoist Master Alfred Huang (2010), Inner Traditions

The Holographic Paradigm and Other Paradoxes, edited by Ken Wilber (1982), Shambhala

The Nine Doors of Midgard, by Edred Thorsson (2018), The Rune-Gild

The Ra Material: The Law of One, by Jim McCarty, Don Elkins and Carla L. Rueckert (1981), Whitford Press

Ancient Teachings on the EGO: In Daphna Moore's Rabbi's Tarot by Daphna Moore, Suzzan Babcock (2016), CreateSpace Independent Publishing Platform

The Soul Source—A Primer for Living as a Soul, by David E Hopper (2015), CreateSpace Independent Publishing Platform

Wheels of Life, by Anodea Smith (1987), Llewellyn's New Age

About the Author

Born to Soviet emigrants in the United Kingdom and as the only Jewish pupil in Catholic schools, Helen was accustomed to not fitting in, which regularly meant observing how other people did. This curiosity remained throughout her studies in neuroscience (BSc), behavioural neuropharmacology (PhD), and ten years of travelling across six continents of our planet.

As a mentor, Helen helps individuals understand why their lives are the way they are, and guides them through personal transformation to realise the far reaches of their capabilities.

You can connect with me on:

🌐 https://thewhiterabbitreveals.com

🔗 https://www.helenmosimannkogan.com

🔗 https://www.linkedin.com/in/helen-mosimann-kogan-50699223a

🔗 http://bio.site/helenmosimannkogan

Subscribe to my newsletter:

✉ https://thewhiterabbitreveals.com/ffahome

Also by Helen Mosimann-Kogan Ph.D.

Helen has never known a time when she hasn't wondered why people, herself included, think, behave and feel the way they do. At her birth, she probably wondered why the doctor that delivered her chose to wear a blue tie that day.

Curious about her own and other people's lives was one thing, then at a crunch point somewhere between 2005 and 2010, Helen realised life on Earth was never going to be the same again. It took a few years to process the implications of this, and many more years to comprehend how this was going to roll out. Call it the awakening, the Shift, the dawn of a new age, global crisis—whatever you will—this would bring a dramatically new storyline to the ways humans think, feel and behave, a storyline that Helen has been keenly exploring ever since.

Helen is interested in unveiling the mysteries and making them accessible to anyone who is interested. Aside from the books below, you can find her most recent writings in the courses available at helenmosimannkogan.com and thewhiterabbitreve als.com—where she brings ancient keys to the modern age for self-reflection and realisation.

The Science of Acting

'To create believable characters the actor has to think the character's thoughts'. This is the premise of this work. However, it begs the question, What does one (the actor in particular) think? How can one think the character's thoughts when one doesn't know what's going on inside their own head?

Enter *The Science of Acting*, a systematic approach for the actor to increase his/her self-awareness and understand the fundamental processes and patterns which govern how we all think. Whether you are playing the role of an acorn or of Hamlet, the subjects covered give the actor the tools and a structured process to confidently repeat a good performance—and the awareness to know what to do to adjust a performance that was less-than. Included is the Ten-Step approach to working with a script, with a one-act Chekhov play example.

'Why would a workable theory of consciousness come out of a drama school and not a laboratory? The answer is that scientists cannot create life situations in the artificial circumstances of a laboratory. In a theatre, we have to create different states of consciousness on a daily basis.'—Sam Kogan

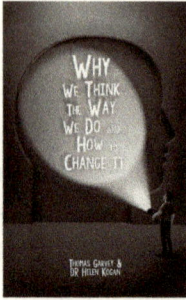

Why We Think the Way We Do and How to Change It

'This book creates an easy-to-read self-help tool. Our aim is to provide you with enough information, in sufficient detail, so that what you read makes sense, you can see it work, and crucially that it makes a difference to your life.'

The Science of Acting (2009) left many readers wanting more, because they knew there was more. Evidently *The Science of Acting* was comprised of more than a technique to act well: included within it were tools to change one's life.

Building on this, together with Thomas Garvey, Dr. Helen Kogan set about writing a book that would solely focus on improving the layperson's life, by helping them understand why their lives play out as they do.

Why We Think the Way We Do and How to Change It hones in on the finest workings of our minds and delves deep to disentangle and dissolve the thoughts and behaviours that hold us back from living fulfilled lives.

Shame, guilt, success, failure, relationships, sex and family dynamics are some of the key areas that are addressed in the chapters dedicated to the origins, patterns and processes of our thinking. In particular, the authors repeatedly return to the question, 'Why is it that although we so desperately want our lives to change, we can't make it happen?' And they answer it, by illustrating the payoffs for staying the same that we cling to—however painful or nonsensical.

Why We Think the Way We Do and How to Change It will take you on an honest journey of self-reflection and understanding, to put your life firmly in your hands—so that you can steer it exactly where you want to go.